101 Surefire Ways to Start the School Year

by Joan Novelli and
Susan Shafer

Cover design by Norma Ortiz
Interior design by Sydney Wright
Illustrations by James G. Hale

ISBN 0-590-36515-0

SCHOLASTIC
PROFESSIONAL BOOKS

New York • Toronto • London • Auckland • Sydney
Mexico City • New Delhi • Hong Kong

Contents

About This Book

There are many ways to approach those first days of school. But whatever your plan, you probably share these goals:

- to build a sense of community;
- to establish routines and boundaries;
- to make children feel comfortable and knowledgeable about the space, materials, and people in the room;
- to help children feel confident about themselves and their ability to learn; and
- to create a learning environment that is inviting and invigorating.

In short, you want to fuel children's excitement about coming to school each day and develop an atmosphere that will help them achieve their goals. This book features activities that can help you do just that. You'll find innovative ways to make: name tags, perfect first-week picture books, unusual icebreakers, engaging first-week I Spy games, collaborative getting-to-know-you books, class graphs, interactive bulletin boards, and more—all designed to help you and your students make your first weeks back the best ever.

Elementary teachers from around the country contributed many of the ideas in this book—ideas that we hope will inspire your teaching, excite your students, and energize your classroom for the first week and beyond!

Niftiest Name Tags

Name tags serve the obvious purpose—helping you and your students get to know one another's names. For young children, they also provide a wonderful foray into reading and writing. Students' names are at the heart of a beginning literacy program. Whenever you use students' names, you build in meaning, strengthening the connections young children make between letters and sounds. Making name tags is a perfect beginning literacy activity that will also let your students know that they are an important part of the class from the start. If you work with older students, you can focus more on creativity—using name tags to tell a little bit about themselves. Whatever your approach, name tags help children get to know their classmates and make them feel a part of their new classroom.

Pick-a-Pocket

Letting children check themselves in each day is a small but important step in building responsibility in the classroom. This pocket board

makes it easy. Assemble the board by cutting strips of oaktag and folding up the bottom third to make a long pocket. Staple every four inches or so to create individual pockets. Make as many strips as necessary to create a pocket for each student. Make name tags by having students draw pictures of themselves and write their names on index cards. Staple an envelope at the top to hold students' tags when not in use. When students come to school in the morning, they can take out their tags and slip them into a pocket.

Me on a Magnet

My students make attendance cards by writing their names and drawing self-portraits on index cards. I laminate the cards, glue a magnet strip onto the back of each (available in craft stores), and set up the morning check-in on a magnetic board. On one half, I write, "Who's here?" On the other half, "Who's not?" When students come in, they move their names to the "Who's here?" side. When I take attendance, I invite a volunteer to read the names of students who are absent. This helps students get to know their classmates' names, as well as learn to recognize them in print.

Paul Oh, Fort River School
Amherst, Massachusetts

Tags With Texture

Offer students fabric and wallpaper scraps to create name tags at the start of the year. They can cut out the letters of their names from the scraps, then paste the letters onto index cards. Laminate the cards for

durability and then punch holes at the top. Screw cup hooks on a board to make an attendance center where children can hang their tags when they come in each morning. Students will enjoy choosing colors and textures that suit their styles, and the result will be a set of name tags as unique as your class!

T·e·a·c·h·e·r S·h·a·r·e

Countertop Tags

Countertop samples make unique and sturdy name tags. (Check local kitchen-and-bath stores or architects and designers for laminated samples.) They're about 2-by-3 inches long and come with prepunched holes at the top. Each student can select a sample, stick on a blank label, and print his or her name on it. (You might prepare them in advance for younger students.) Screw cup hooks into a board to make a check-in board where students can hang their tags in the morning.

Cathi Farrington, Orchard School
South Burlington, Vermont

Rebus Name Tags

Don't just write your name on the board for students to learn. Help them remember it by writing it as a rebus. For example, "Mrs. Einhorn" could be (picture of eye) + n + (picture of horn). Let children try to make their own name tags with rebus puzzles. You might have them team up so they can help each other out.

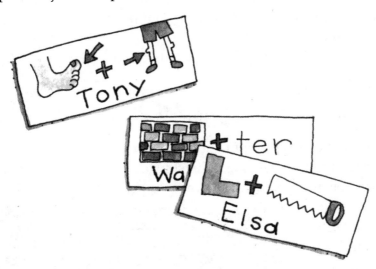

You Make Mine, I'll Make Yours

Pair students on the first day of school to make name tags. Provide index cards and assorted art supplies, and let children make tags for their partners. (Children can spell their names for their partners.) Laminate the tags, punch two holes at the top, and string with yarn. Children can wear their tags around their necks, hanging them up on their coat hooks at the end of the day.

Names by the Dozens

From cubbies to folders and the papers inside, all sorts of things need name tags. Here's a quick-and-easy solution that builds students' name-writing skills at the same time. At the beginning of the year, give each student a sheet of stick-on name tags. Have children write their names on the tags and decorate them if desired. (You could also do this on the computer using a program like *Kid Pix* and printing on labels.) File the name tags you don't use right off the bat, and dip into them as the need arises—for example, using them to label bulletin-board projects, portfolios, and so on.

TIP

Take the name tag notion further by letting students create labels for things in the room—book shelves (tags can show which books go where), marker holders, community-pencil boxes, drawing paper, writing paper, and so on. These kinds of labels will reduce disruption and facilitate everyday routines throughout the year.

Some teachers ask children to label their own cubbies, giving children ownership and responsibility for their space.

First-Week Read-Alouds

Books are filled with friendly and familiar faces just waiting to welcome your new students back to school. Summaries and suggested extension activities for these and other wonderful titles follow.

That Dreadful Day
James Stevenson
(Greenwillow, 1985)
Grandpa tells about his first—and worst—day at school. Other books in this series include *Worse Than Willy!*, *Could Be Worse*, and *What's Under My Bed?*, each of which features stories from Grandpa's childhood.

■ TRY THIS ■

Invite parents, grandparents, big brothers and sisters, and school staff to visit your class to tell their first-day-of-school stories. Take a vote: Who had the worst day? The best? Invite children to tell something that happened on their first day of school. Write each child's story on a piece of paper. Have children illustrate their stories. Put pages together to make a book.

Relaxing About Learning

Leo the Late Bloomer by Robert Kraus (HarperCollins) is a reassuring story for the beginning of the year. It reminds children that everybody learns at different rates and it's okay if the child next to you is reading *War and Peace* while you just started *The Cat in the Hat.*

Bob Krech, Dutch Neck School
Princeton Junction, New Jersey

Feelings
Aliki
(William Morrow, 1986)
A perfect companion to any of the books on the list here, this picture book introduces a range of emotions.

■ TRY THIS ■

Reread the book, letting children stop you when they recognize a feeling they've experienced and share their stories. Act out some of the vignettes in the story to further explore feelings.

Where Are You Going, Manyoni?
Catherine Stock
(William Morrow, 1993)
Manyoni doesn't take a bus, subway, car, or cab to school. She walks. The trip to school for Manyoni and her friends is about two hours. Tag along on that walk with this story and take a look at a child's life in Zimbabwe, where Manyoni lives.

■ TRY THIS ■

How do your students get to school, and what do they pass on the way? After giving children a few days to make observations on their way to and from school, have them put together picture books about getting to school. (Or have each child write and illustrate a page for a class book.) For a class graph connection, see How Do You Get to School?, page 48.

Today Was a Terrible Day
Patricia Reilly Giff
(Viking, 1980)
Second grade is a struggle for Ronald Morgan, who thinks he can't read. Ronald also appears in *Watch Out, Ronald Morgan!*, *Ronald Morgan Goes to Bat*, and *The Almost Funny Play*.

■ TRY THIS ■

Your students each have their own strengths—whether it's reading or keeping a cubby neat and clean. Celebrate these individual strengths by starting an "I Can" list display. Cover a bulletin board with craft paper. Hang up chart paper and provide a box of markers. At the top of the chart paper, write the words: "I CAN…" Start the chart by inviting a student to say something she is good at. Add it to the chart, and have the child sign her name. (You can also have students do this for one another.) As children add to the list, take time to read new comments and recognize students' strengths.

T·e·a·c·h·e·r S·h·a·r·e

Butterflies and Other Feelings
I read aloud *Will I Have a Friend?* by Miriam Cohen (Macmillan, 1967) to help children talk about first-day feelings. Before we read, I share some of my own feelings. Children seem to take comfort in knowing teachers get butterflies in their stomachs too!

Linda Cardoza, Ascarate Elementary
El Paso, Texas

Timothy Goes to School
Rosemary Wells
(Dial, 1981)

Timothy, a raccoon, doesn't quite have
the first day of school he had hoped for—
and he's in tears when he gets home at
the end of the day. Then he meets a new
friend, and things look up.

■ TRY THIS ■

Most of us can relate to the themes in this story of fitting in and finding
friends. Reread the beginning of the book, asking children to pay close
attention to the pictures. Then take another look at the ending. What
are some of the picture clues that tell students how Timothy is feeling?
Use the book as a springboard to discussing students' first-day feelings.
Introduce new vocabulary for feelings. List the words on a chart, leav-
ing room for illustrations. Let children work in teams to illustrate each
feeling. Glue illustrations to the chart, and display. Encourage children
to use the words and pictures to help describe how they're feeling at
different times during the day.

Chrysanthemum
Kevin Henkes
(Greenwillow, 1991)

Chrysanthemum leads a charmed life from the day she's born—until
she starts school. When the teacher takes attendance,
Chrysanthemum's name is met with giggles and unkind remarks: "It's
so long," "It scarcely fits on your name tag," "You're named after a
flower!" Chrysanthemum decides school isn't the place for her. But
then the other children learn that their beloved music teacher's name is
Delphinium. And everything changes.

■ TRY THIS ■

Have children count the number of letters in their names. Set up a graph to record the data. Children can print their names on index cards and tape them in the correct column to show how many letters they have. What is the shortest name? Longest? How many names have more than three letters? Fewer than three? How many names have exactly five letters? Ten? Invite children to ask questions based on the graph too. Translate the data into a live graph, having children line up in rows according to the number of letters in their names. (For a related activity, see Numbers in Your Name, page 47.)

T·e·a·c·h·e·r S·h·a·r·e

School Supplies

The sharp points of brand-new crayons, the clean white paper in new notebooks… these are familiar signs of a new school year for me. To capture the fresh feeling of a new year, I share poems from *School Supplies*, edited by Lee Bennett Hopkins and Renee Flowers (Simon & Schuster Children's, 1996). New Notebook by Judith Thurman ("Lines in a new notebook run, even and fine, like telephone wires across a shadowy landscape…") is great fun as a read-aloud. I follow up by inviting students to write their own poems based on the new supplies they'll share in their classroom.

Judy Vowels, Hazelwood Elementary
Louisville, Kentucky

Moog-Moog, Space Barber
Mark Teague
(Scholastic, 1991)
Like so many children, Elmo Freem gets a haircut before heading back to school. But the barber's skills leave something to be desired: "Even Elmo's baseball cap couldn't cover up the problem." Needless to say,

Elmo is not looking forward to his first day back. But then some space monsters come to the rescue. Well, they try anyway, but not even the great Moog, space barber extraordinaire, can help. The first day of school arrives. As Elmo sits worrying about his hair, his friend Buford shows up. And guess what? He's got a stocking cap on too!

■ TRY THIS ■

Whether it's a bad haircut or some other cause of concern, children have plenty to worry about when they start school. Sometimes just knowing that another child shares the same problem can help. Invite children to write down their fears on slips of paper (or dictate them). Pull them out one at a time and share them aloud. How many children worry about the same thing?

T·e·a·c·h·e·r S·h·a·r·e

Organizing Your Class Library

One thing I don't get ready before the start of school is our class library. Letting my students organize the books is a great way to bring the class together and help them know that the library is really theirs.

• I start by piling books into five cardboard boxes and telling children that they are going to help set up the class library.

• We discuss categories for sorting the books. As children make suggestions, I ask them to think about whether it will be easy to find a book within that category.

• After agreeing on a final set of categories, children form groups of five and start sorting. They use stick-on notes to label the books. Over a couple of days, we get the books sorted and shelved. By the end of this project, my students feel a part of the classroom and really know their books!   *Shoshana Jacobs, P.S. 163*
New York, New York

Miss Bindergarten Gets Ready for Kindergarten
Joseph Slate
(Dutton, 1996)
"Adam Krupp wakes up. Brenda Heath brushes her teeth...Miss Bindergarten gets ready for kindergarten." Like meeting their teachers in the grocery store and being surprised to see them out of the classroom, children will be amused by what's going on in Miss Bindergarten's life while her students are getting ready for school.

■ TRY THIS ■

Play a game of "I'm Getting Ready." Have children take turns telling their name and something they do to get ready for school. (Elena puts on her favorite sneakers.) Of course, you have to take a turn too, sharing something you do to get ready for your day. Students' responses will make a wonderful book for your class library. You might audiotape the responses and transcribe them later.

Anabelle Swift, Kindergartner
Amy Schwartz
(Orchard Books, 1988)
Anabelle gets some advice from her big sister, Lucy, about all the things she needs to know the first day of school.

■ TRY THIS ■

Bring students together to write an official guide to your grade. In the short amount of time students have been in school, what tips would they pass along to a new student? Children will pick up helpful hints from one another as they share information and advice. They'll gain confidence too, as they see how much they already know about their new grade. If this is your students' second or third year in school, make a guide for a class of younger kids.

Lunch Bunnies
By Kathryn Lasky
(Little Brown, 1996)

It's Clyde's first day of school, and he's okay
with everything but lunch. It doesn't help that
his older brother teases him. "You better hope
they don't have soup," he tells Clyde. And
then there's always "mystery goosh" to worry
about. Clyde feels a lot better when he meets
Rosemary in the lunch line. But will they
make it to the table holding their trays without an incident?

■ TRY THIS ■

This book begs for a follow-up that lets students practice their cafeteria
skills. Borrow some trays from the cafeteria and let students load them
up and walk from one place to another. Have children team up and
take turns acting as cafeteria worker and student. They can pay for
lunch with pretend money or tickets

T·e·a·c·h·e·r S·h·a·r·e

Reading Response Sheets

Reprinted response sheets make it easy for children to develop good
reading habits from the start. When my students finish a book (reading
pictures and/or words), they complete a response sheet, then file their
papers in folders. This procedure lets them know from the beginning
that reading is important—especially their thoughts about what they
read. Offering a selection of response sheets builds variety and choice
into the activity. (See sample response sheets, next page.)

Diane Farnham, Orchard School
South Burlington, Vermont

Reading Response Sheet

Name _____ Date _____

Book Title _____

Author _____

Illustrator _____

Color the face that
shows what you thought
of the story.

What is something you would tell a friend about the
story? _____

_____

_____

Reading Response Sheet

Name _____ Date _____

I read a book called _____

This book was written by _____

This book was illustrated by _____

I think the book is _____ fiction _____ nonfiction

This is why I think so. _____

_____

_____

_____

_____

Ready to Read
Young children are often told by parents, aunts, uncles, older brothers and sisters, and grandparents that when they get to first grade they "will learn how to read." Since learning to read doesn't happen on the first (or second!) day, I try to present something that everyone can read. *Deep in the Forest* by Brinton Turkle (Dutton,1976) is a wordless adaptation of Goldilocks with a twist—the bear goes to the girl's cabin. The children are usually familiar with the story of Goldilocks and enjoy reading this variation. I offer other twists on this tale too, including my favorite, *Somebody and the Three Blairs* by Marilyn Tolhurst (Orchard Books,1990).
Charlotte Sassman, Alice Carlson Applied Learning Center
Fort Worth, Texas

Minerva Louise at School
Janet Morgan Stoeke
(Dutton, 1996)
If your students' spirits need a boost—even if they don't—share this book about a hen who thinks the school is her barn and the kids' cubbies her nesting boxes.

■ TRY THIS ■

Read other books about Minerva, including *Minerva Louise* and *A Hat for Minerva Louise*. Start a character web about Minerva. What words can students use to describe her? What qualities do they notice in each of the books? Team up students to make webs about each other. (Or do this as a class activity, making a couple of webs each day.)

School Daze
Charles Keller
(Prentice Hall, 1981)
These dialogue jokes are just right for reading aloud in class and providing a daily dose of humor.

■ TRY THIS ■

Write children's names on slips of paper and put them in a bag. Each day, invite a volunteer to come up and select a name from the bag. Have these children team up to "perform" a joke.

T·e·a·c·h·e·r S·h·a·r·e

Portrait of a Friend

Oliver Button Is a Sissy by Tomie dePaolo (Harcourt Brace, 1979) tells the story of a boy who doesn't quite fit in. He doesn't like sports, preferring reading and painting pictures. He's good at tap dancing too. This story is a wonderful springboard for talking about the ways students are alike and different. It's a good opportunity to talk about teasing, too—perhaps brainstorming things kids can do when it happens to them.

As a way to help students further appreciate one another's differences, we set up a "portrait studio" bulletin board. We cover the board with craft paper, add a border, then tack up a pad of large paper and a basket of markers, crayons, and colored pencils. Children visit the display in pairs and draw one another's portraits. I encourage children to pay attention to the details that make each of them unique. Some have curly hair, others straight. Some wear glasses, others don't. Students add words to the portraits that describe their partners—for example, Anna likes baseball and ballet. She doesn't like pizza! We display finished portraits around the room.

Judy Meagher, Emily Dickenson School, Bozeman, Montana

Arthur's Teacher Trouble
Marc Brown
(Little Brown, 1987)
Arthur's got a bad feeling about his new teacher, Mr. Ratburn. Not only are the students in his

class excused in alphabetical order, but they have homework the first day! Then comes the 100-word spelling test…

■ TRY THIS ■

What would your students say about a 100-word spelling test? Hold a spell-a-thon, just for fun. Use words from a theme unit or other class activity (weather words, etc.). Let children play different roles in the spell-a-thon. Some may prefer to help organize the event rather than take a turn spelling words. Others can do the principal's job in the story—read the words the children have to spell and provide definitions.

The First Grade Takes a Test
Miriam Cohen
(Greenwillow, 1980)
Get together with Anna Maria, Jim, Alex, and the other friends in this popular series to find out about life in first grade. Other books in the series include *See You in Second Grade!*

■ TRY THIS ■

Before you read, ask your first graders what they think life in first grade will be like. After reading, invite a few of your students from last year to visit and talk with your class about the first grade they remember. Ask your new students to add things they already like about first (or whatever) grade.

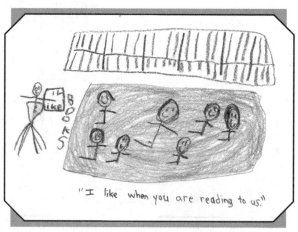

"I like when you are reading to us."

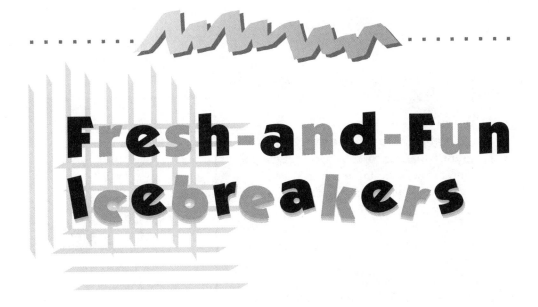

Fresh-and-Fun Icebreakers

Children often warm up to one another very quickly. But there's no harm in helping them along at the start of a new school year. Besides, who wouldn't want to play these fun get-to-know-you games? Use them to begin to create bonds in your classroom that will encourage a spirit of friendship and cooperation that will last the year.

Pass the Popcorn

Pass around a bowl of popcorn or mini-pretzel sticks. Ask children to wait until you say it's okay to eat the snack. After everyone has some, have children count the pieces of popcorn (or pretzels) in their hands. One at a time, invite children to tell about themselves—sharing one thing for each piece of popcorn they have. (For example, a child with eight pieces of popcorn will tell eight things about himself.) To take the idea further, record children's comments on chart paper, one child per page. Put the pages together and bind on the left or at the top to make a class book of mini-autobiographies.

Team Tic-Tac-Toe

This icebreaker puts a tic-tac-toe twist on the usual get-to-know-you scavenger hunt. I make a tic-tac-toe board on a regular 8½-by-11-inch sheet of paper and at the top, write: "Find someone who…." In each square, I write a mathematical prompt. Here are some examples:

Find someone who…

… has three pockets.

… is wearing six circles (buttons, shoelace eyelets, etc.).

… has a phone number that adds up to a number less than 25.

… has five people in her family.

… has nine letters in his name.

… has the same number of letters in her name as you.

Children mingle with classmates, looking for those who fit the descriptions in the boxes. When they find someone who does, they ask this person to write his name in the box. At the same time, children who fit the descriptions can look for children who need their squares signed. In the process, students have fun, do math, and learn one another's names. You can easily alter this activity for any grade by changing the level of difficulty of the math prompts.

Bob Krech, Dutch Neck School
Princeton Junction, New Jersey

Catch That Name

Get a softball, and gather students in a circle to play a get-to-know-you game. Start by giving one child the ball and asking her to throw it to you. When you catch it, say the name of the person who threw you the ball, then say your name. Now pass the ball to another student and have that child say your name and his name. Continue until all children have had a chance to catch the ball.

All Aboard

Children add cars to a human train as they learn one another's names. To play, have children stand together in a circle. Ask one child to introduce herself, then say, "Who are you?" to a classmate. ("Hi, I'm Una. Who are you?") The second child responds with "Hi, Una. I'm Corina." The human train repeats that name like the steam blasts on a choo-choo train ("Corina. Corina. Corina."). Corina holds on to the leader's waist and the train moves to another child. The game continues until introductions are made, names are repeated, and there's one long train.

Class Connections

Play this game to help a new group of students see how much they have in common.
- Start by saying something about yourself. ("This summer, I went camping in Canada.")
- Invite a student to follow up with a new sentence that makes a connection with yours. ("My aunt lives in Canada.")
- Let the next child make another connection. ("My aunt came to visit me on my birthday.")

- Continue until as many students who want to have made a connection (or until students can't make any more connections). Provide prompts as necessary to help students think of possible connections.

—Adapted from "The Caring Classroom: We're All in This Together" by William J. Kreidler (Instructor, October 1995)

I'm a Mystery

Cut strips of paper to fit around students' heads. Give one to each student. Have children print their names on the strips. Place the strips in a paper bag. Have children take turns selecting a strip with eyes closed. Wrap the strip around the child's head with the name facing out, and tape in place. Have the child wearing the headband ask classmates "yes or no" questions about the identity of the child whose name is on the strip—for example, "Am I a girl? Do I have brown hair? Do I have freckles?" Let the child guess the identity up to three times, then reveal it, and let another child take a turn.

—Adapted from Super Start-the-School-Year Book *by Meish Goldish (Scholastic Professional Books, 1991), a collection of games, bulletin boards, plays, and more.*

A Bag About Us

Ask children to each bring in an item that tells something about themselves and place it (secretly) in a large class bag. Each morning during the first few weeks of school, pull out one item. Can anyone guess who it belongs to? Let a few children guess before asking the owner to reveal herself. Have this child tell his or her name and a little bit about the item. ("My name is Annie Rose. This is a picture of my cat, Pete. We got Pete from the animal shelter when we lived in our other house.") After everyone has had a chance to talk (do a few introductions per day), display the objects and let students try to identify their owners. ("That's Masami's origami frog!")

T·e·a·c·h·e·r S·h·a·r·e

Round and Round

This game pairs students off with their classmates—one at a time—until everyone has met one another. To start, students form two circles, an inner circle and an outer circle. Circles face each other, and children pair off in twos. Each child in the inner circle asks a question about the facing child in the outer circle, then they switch. Example: Child A (inner circle): "Do you like dogs?" Child B (outer circle): "Yes, I have three!" Child B: "What's your favorite sport?" Child A: "I like to play soccer." Now the inner circle moves clockwise by one child. Each child faces a new partner. The new pair exchanges questions and answers, then the inner circle moves on again. This repeats until each child has asked everyone in the outer circle a question.

Shoshana Jacobs, P.S. 163
New York, New York

Name Tag

Make a name tag for each child. Divide the class into two groups. Give each child in group A a name tag of one of the children in group B. Have children move about, trying to match name tags to classmates. As children in group A find matching children in group B, they stand still together. Play until all children have been tagged, and then play again, this time giving children in group B the name tags.

Bish Bosh

Bring children together in a circle. Have one child begin by pointing to another child and saying either *bish* or *bosh*. If this child says *bish*, the child whom he pointed to must tell the name of the classmate to the left. If this child says *bosh*, the child she pointed to tells the name of the classmate to the right. The child who was pointed to takes over, pointing to another child and saying either *bish* or *bosh*. The game continues until all children have had a chance to name a classmate. Tip: This is a good time to review directionals *left* and *right*.

Animal Size Order

This cooperative learning game is best played in small groups of eight to ten—though you can certainly play with the entire class. Give each child a card on which you've written the name of an animal, such as tiger, giraffe, or elephant. Draw or paste a picture of each animal on the cards to provide visual clues for beginning readers. Have children put themselves in size order from smallest to largest, without talking!

Where in the Classroom?

To help children get to know one another and their classroom, I team them up for a scavenger hunt of things in the room—the attendance chart, scissors, pencils, pencil sharpener, games, books, tissues, and so on. Children work in pairs to complete the hunt. Matching up children who don't know each other yet gives everyone a chance to get acquainted. Students check off each item as they find it.

Shoshana Jacobs
P.S. 163
New York, New York

Name _____

Partner's Name _____

Can you find:

___ 1. the attendance chart

___ 2. a pair of scissors

___ 3. paints and paintbrushes

___ 4. a box of tissues

___ 5. books you can read

___ 6. paper you can write on

___ 7. pencils you can write with

___ 8. a pencil sharpener

___ 9. games to play

___ 10. a folder with your name on it

An Animal Like Me

Make sets of animal name cards by writing the name of each animal on two cards. (So, for example, write *dog* on two cards, *cow* on two cards, and so on.) You'll need one card for each child. Give children a card and have them wander around the room, making the sounds of their animals. When children find their animal match, have them sit down. When all children have found their partners, have each pair make the sound one more time, while the class identifies the animal.

Make a Switch

Sitting in pairs, have children study their partners' attire for one minute. Then have one child in each pair close his eyes, while the other changes one small detail—for example, removing eyeglasses or rolling up a sleeve. Can the other child identify the change? Play this game several times, mixing up partners so that children get to play with a few different classmates.

It's a Puzzle

Take photos of groups of four children. Paste photos on poster board and write the children's names on the back. Cut the poster board into irregularly shaped pieces, making a jigsaw puzzle. Let each group work on another group's puzzle, trying to put the pieces together, familiarizing themselves with their classmates' faces and names as they work.

Start the Year Scavenger Hunt

A familiar icebreaker, you can keep get-to-know-you scavenger hunts fresh by varying the things children have to find. You can prepare a scavenger hunt record sheet such as the one at the right. Encourage children to find a different child, if possible, for each item.

Find a classmate who:
___ has ridden in an airplane;
___ has twins in the family;
___ loves spaghetti;
___ wears glasses;
___ has a collection;
___ has a birthday this month;
___ has more than five letters in his
    or her first name;
___ can hop on one foot ten times
    without stopping;
___ is wearing red today;
___ can say a word in another language.

Unity-Builders

What does unity in a classroom look like? It's a spirit of cooperation among a teacher and group of students. It's the way children care about and help one another. It's a sense of belonging that children feel about their classroom—and the people in it. It's listening to one another and respecting different ideas. It's sharing responsibilities. It's families involved in classroom activities and their children's growth as learners, and more. Building unity in a classroom can begin on day one—and can weave its way into almost everything you do. The activities here can help too—offering specific ways to set a group-building tone for the year and to help children develop ownership and pride in their classroom.

T·e·a·c·h·e·r S·h·a·r·e

Kiva in the Classroom
Kiva is an American Indian word for *community*. Our first activity of the year is a kiva that focuses on community building and getting along with each other. Our intent is to value individuals and honor diversity. We sit in a big circle and pass around a little ball. Each child holds the ball over his head and tells what can he or she can do to cooperate, then

passes the ball to the next person.

Marci Halperin, Celebration School
Celebration, Florida

Class Name
A class name can help children develop a sense of belonging. We brainstorm possible names together, names that convey children's strengths as a class of learners, such as the Brainy Bunch, Super-duper Stars, or Awesome Authors. Voting on a name builds enthusiasm, autonomy, and responsibility—and makes using the name more meaningful to students.

In addition to posting the class name on our door, we make it part of our yearlong activities. For example, we add it to notes that go home (Sincerely, [your name] and the Brainy Bunch) and sign it to letters we write to other classes. (Come see the aquarium exhibit in our room tomorrow at noon. —The Science Stars). Rather than being "Mrs. Sullivan's class," students have a class identity that expresses who they are as a group.

Karen Sullivan, George Washington Elementary
Mt. Vernon, New York

Morning Message
Who doesn't love getting letters? I write my students a "morning message" each day, sharing news about the day, complimenting them on their accomplishments, and so on. They sign their names at the bottom to let me know they've read it (or listened to a classmate read it). My students really look forward to their "letter" each day. It's a warm way to start the day and bring everyone together.

Paul Oh, Fort River School
Amherst, Massachusetts

Linking Letters

Play a Scrabble-like game that invites students to link their names together, one at a time. Start by making a large grid. (Make the squares big enough for students to see from where they are sitting.) Invite a child to write his or her name on the grid, one letter per square. Ask children to think about whether their names have any letters in common with the first child's name. Choose a student who does have letters in common to write his name on the grid, linking the names by one letter either horizontally or vertically. Continue until all children have had a chance to add their names to the grid. Display the linking names.

B	E	N										
	L											
	L	I	L	L	Y							
	E		E									
	N		O	N	A			D				
					N		K	A	M	I	L	
					Y			M				
					A	L	I	C	I	A		

T·e·a·c·h·e·r   S·h·a·r·e

Time-Capsule Tubes

Collecting baseline data about children's abilities is a focus of mine during the first weeks of school. I want to know where each child starts academically so that I can chart her growth during the year. As I administer various assessment tools, such as Marie Clay's Observational Survey, math and science interest surveys, and so on, I share the purpose with children—that what we are doing will help us see how much they already know and, at the end of the year, how much they've grown. This leads to a discussion of time capsules and the way that a time capsule freezes a moment in time. I read Aliki's *Digging Up Dinosaurs* (HarperCollins, 1981) and show the *Reading Rainbow* videotape of the book, in which a time capsule is buried. We follow up by making time capsules about ourselves, using bathroom-tissue tubes. Some of the things children include are:

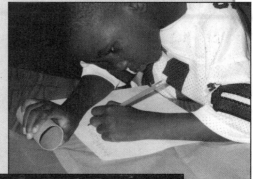

- outlines of their hands (children help one another with tracing, building community as we work);
- their names in the best possible handwriting (often they can't spell their last name, so there is my next lesson);
- a list of favorites (foods, colors, books, and so on);
- a piece of yarn as tall as they are (they work together to measure each other).

They stuff all of this into their bathroom-tissue tubes, wrap the tubes in tissue paper, and twist the ends, fire-cracker style. We "bury" the tubes in a paper sack and write, Do Not Open Until the Last Day of School on the bag. I make a big deal of sealing the bag with masking tape. We place the bag on top of a cabinet where we can see it every

day. During the year, the children often remind one another, "Not until the last day of school!" This activity is a great way to develop community and give the children something to look forward to at the end of the school year.

Charlotte Sassman, Alice Carlson Applied Learning Center
Fort Worth, Texas

First-Week
I Spy Games

The *I Spy* series by Jean Marzollo and Walter Wick is a favorite with children of all ages. Like others in the series, *I Spy School Days* (Scholastic, 1995) is full of inventive photos and playful riddles that invite children to find all sorts of hidden objects. At the back of *I Spy School Days*, Jean and Walter explain the inspiration for their book. They had visited schools where children were busy making their own *I Spy* projects and decided to create a new *I Spy* book to celebrate the "joy of intellectual discovery" they saw in these children. The book includes pages on chalkboard fun; patterns and paint; the playground; mapping, sorting, and classifying, and more—each one full of discoveries in the making. Use the activities here to launch your own I Spy activities for the first week and beyond.

I Spy Bookshelf

I Spy Bookshelf
In addition to *I Spy: School Days*, books in the I Spy series include:
I Spy: A Book of Picture Riddles
I Spy Christmas: A Book of Picture Riddles
I Spy Funhouse: A Book of Picture Riddles
I Spy Mystery: A Book of Picture Riddles
I Spy Fantasy: A Book of Picture Riddles
I Spy Spooky Nights: A Book of Picture Riddles
I Spy Little Animals
I Spy Little Book
I Spy Little Wheels

If you and your students have access to a computer, you'll love *I Spy: Brain-Building Games for Kids* (Scholastic), available on CD-ROM for Macintosh and Windows.

T·e·a·c·h·e·r S·h·a·r·e

I Spy

We make our own I Spy class book that lets each child get to know the "little stuff" in our classroom—Legos, unifix cubes, scissors, multi-links, snap blocks, crayons, paper clips, and so on. Each child builds a structure or collage from these materials on a construction-paper background. They use the *I Spy* books for inspiration on how to position their objects and learn a lot about composition in the process. I

use a Polaroid to take a picture of each child's I Spy picture. Children get very involved in telling me how to get just the right angle. Then they compose riddles to go with their pictures.

Charlotte Sassman
Alice Carlson Applied Learning Center
Fort Worth, Texas

I Spy Shapes

Let children explore their new classroom with a series of I Spy shape hunts. Cut out "spy glasses" from oaktag that have openings in different geometric shapes. One day, hunt for triangles with the triangle spy glasses. Another day try circles or squares. Have children hunt for the shapes by walking around the room with their spy glasses. When they discover a shape they can say, "I spy a …" and draw a picture of what they see or list the places they see them. Talk with

children about their discoveries: "How do you know that's a triangle (square, circle, rectangle)? How many sides do you see? Extend the activity by taking children on a walk around the school (inside and/or out) to explore shapes in more places. Let students take their spy glasses home to play I Spy Shapes with their families.

I Spy a Writer

I purchase small magnifying glasses on strings that students can wear as necklaces. (Check a party-supply store. For mail-order, check Constructive Playthings, (800) 832-0224). One of the ways I use the magnifiers is to inspire students' use of detail in their writing. They use the magnifiers to "spy" details around them and then incorporate these into first-week stories. The idea of using a magnifier reminds children to take a close look—just the way they do in the I Spy books—and this is reflected in the use of detail in their writing.

Charlotte Sassman, Alice Carlson Applied Learning Center
Fort Worth, Texas

I Spy ABC's

If assessing students' alphabet skills is part of your beginning-of-the-year tasks, try an I Spy game that invites children to look for objects around the room that start with each letter of the alphabet. (Even children who already have the alphabet down pat will enjoy this game.) Pair children who have early-reading skills in place with children who are just learning to recognize letter-sound relationships. Both children will benefit from the partnership. Have children either collect items in a bag, write down the names of what they find, or draw pictures. This activity might take place over a few days, with children sharing their finds at the end.

I Spy 123's

Get a first-week feel for students' number sense with an I Spy counting game. For young children, you might start with numbers 1 through 10. Team up children, trying to match students who have strong math skills with children who may need assistance. Have them go around the room and try to "spy" something for each number—for example, I spy 1 teacher, 2 *I Spy* books, 3 computers, 4 computer programs, 5 children whose names start with the letter P, 6 tables, 7 windows, 8 charts, 9 boxes of crayons, 10 red folders.

I Spy Your Name

Write each child's name on a slip of paper, and place it in a bag. Have children draw names of classmates and then go around the room and find objects that start with each letter of the child's name. For example, a child who drew *Ben* might find a book, an eraser, and a notebook.

I-Spy-a-Day

Surprise your students each day with an I Spy riddle that challenges them to find something in the classroom (a child or an object). Post the riddle on chart paper or make sentence strips. Cover a shoe box with colorful paper and make a slit in the top. When students think they have solved the I Spy riddle, have them write their answers on paper and put them in the box. At the end of the day or week, reveal the answer you had in mind. You might be surprised at the many other possible answers students found on their own.

I spy a window, a chair, and a pen,
A picture, a plant, and the number 10.

(Children find the number 10.)

Collaborative Getting-to-Know-You Books

The idea of writing, illustrating, and publishing books with children may be more than you want to tackle at the beginning of the year. But collaborative books put all of your students' creative energy into one book. The result? Students develop a spirit of cooperation and pride in what they can do when they work together on a project. Best of all, students will return to their books for weeks, even months, to come.

T·e·a·c·h·e·r S·h·a·r·e

I Can Read
For the very first day of school, I make a booklet for each child (card stock cover and two pages of paper stapled inside) in the shape of a school with a door on the front and the name of our school written across the top. I help children cut the cover to

make the door open (they then get to use those new scissors they brought). Next, they draw themselves and write their names on the first page. Of course, they can read that first page with their names, and I gush on and on about how smart they are, reading the book all by themselves! On the remaining pages, they:

• draw a picture of me and write my name;

• draw/write about a picture of a friend in the class (the friend writes his or her name);

• draw and/or write about a favorite school activity.

They read their books to one another, and soon they know everyone's name. Students take their first-day books home and read them to their parents, brothers, sisters, and so on. I attach a letter explaining what the pages say and how parents can participate in the "reading." These little books do a lot that first day—including convincing my young readers that they can read!

Charlotte Sassman, Alice Carlson Applied Learning Center
Fort Worth, Texas

We're All Experts

Build confidence and cooperation from the start with a picture directory that highlights a skill each child excels in. Start by photocopying a picture of each student (or having children draw pictures of themselves). Have each child paste the picture to a sentence strip, print her name, then write (or dictate) one thing she is good at—for example, building with blocks, working with numbers, reading, writing, using the computer, solving problems, making friends, and so on. Punch holes at the top left and right of each sentence strip and use O-rings to bind. Share the directory with the class, letting each child read his own page. Encourage students to use it on their own when they need help from an expert!

Remember When...

If you teach first grade or beyond, bring students together to write a book of memories. Start by asking students to share their memories from the year before. Record comments on chart paper. When students are finished, cut apart the chart paper so that each student has his sentence. Have children copy their sentences on paper and illustrate them. Bind pages to make a book of memories. Read the book aloud, letting students take turns reading their pages.

Do You Remember When...

A Book of First Grade Memories

By: 1st Grade 220 1996-1997

Organize a memory book at the start of the year around activities such as building, learning to read, meeting new friends, and so on.

Animal Alphabet Book

Combine early literacy skills, art, and a little science with an alphabet book of animals from A to Z. Start by listing students' names on chart paper. Then brainstorm animals that have names that start with the same first letter of each child's name—for example, Angela Alligator, Ben Bear, Camisha Cobra. Have each child write and illustrate a page for the alphabet book. (Some letters might have more than one page.) Work together to make pages with letters of the alphabet that don't match anyone's name. Or send the partially completed book home with a different child each night to see if family members can help out by completing missing pages that correspond to the first letters of their names.

Froggy Wants a Letter

I have a puppet, Froggy, who comes out to meet the class at the beginning of the year. Our first writing piece is always a letter that the puppet demands that the children write to him. (He is rather bossy and arrogant, though deep down he is a softy.) In this letter they tell the puppet about themselves and get to ask him a question. He writes back answering the question. The second time around, after they get to know him a little better, he demands they write a book about him. Each child writes a story about Froggy. The stories are put together and the book is titled, "The Froggy Book." Students then read their stories to Froggy and the book becomes a widely read volume in our class library.

Bob Krech, Dutch Neck School
Princeton Junction, New Jersey

Our Book of Memories

Start the beginning of the year with a memory book you can add to throughout the year. This is a book students will return to again and again to revisit favorite activities and special times. Parents will appreciate it, too.

• Use a commercial scrapbook or use O-rings to bind sturdy paper.

• Have children work together to create a cover. You might pass the book around and have each child write her name on the cover and/or draw a picture. You could also place the book at your writing center and let children visit at different times to add their touch to the cover. Or use a class photo on the cover, and let children sign their names.

- Together list the months of the school year. Help children make tabbed pages for each month. Leave plenty of blank paper in-between each month.

- Let students make their first entry in the book. Toward the end of Day 1, give each child a small piece of paper. Ask children to think about the first day of school and write down (or dictate) something about a memorable moment ("I had butterflies in my stomach until I found out that my pal Willie is in my class. —Larry"). Paste the papers on the first pages of the memory book.

- Continue adding to the memory book with photos, pictures, stories, mementos, and so on. Be sure to take time during the year to look back on what students have done. Encourage children to share the book with parents when they visit.

Class Address Book

Help every child feel like a part of the class by putting together a class address book. Unlike the ones that just list students' names, phone numbers, and addresses, this version lets each child create an illustrated page.

- Obtain parents' permission before including any child's name, address, or phone number. (You can still include each child in the book. Just leave out information a parent might not want to have published.)

- Use the address book form on page 43 to get started. Have children complete the information at the top, then illustrate with a self-portrait (or photo), and a picture of home.

- Photocopy the pages and put together a book for each child. Children will be excited to see themselves in the books, and they'll easily be able to get in touch with classmates for play dates or homework help.

	Name _____
	Address _____
	_____
	_____
	_____
	Phone _____
	e-mail _____

Back-to-School Bus

Celebrate school with this interactive bus-shaped book.

- Draw a full-page outline of a school bus. Copy the following poem on the inside of the outline.

Back to School
School! School! Here we come,
Lots to learn and so much fun.
Working, playing, all day through,
And here's my favorite thing to do:

_____
_____

- Photocopy a class set of the pages and give one to each child.

- Read aloud the poem, completing it by saying something you like to do at school. Reread the poem, asking children to join in. When you get to the last line, let children take turns saying something they like to do at school.

- Have children complete their pages by using words or pictures to tell their favorite thing to do.
- Instruct children to cut out the bus shape. Put pages together and add a front cover and back cover. If you want to get fancy, use paper fasteners to attach wheels to the front and back covers, or to each page. Watch them spin! Staple pages together (or bind with yarn) to make a book.

Note: This activity was adapted from *Collaborative Books to Make and Share* by Mary Beth Spann (Scholastic Professional Books, 1997). In addition to this back-to-school bus book, you'll find suggestions and templates for making and sharing collaborative books about clocks, castles, weather, pumpkins, penguins, and more—30 in all!

T·e·a·c·h·e·r   S·h·a·r·e

First Words and Pictures

Early in September, we ask children to draw a picture of "someone or something they know and care about." We ask children to label their pictures and explain what's going on there. (Example: "My mommy takes me to the school bus.")

You can use these pictures as an informal writing assessment tool. (Look for scribbles, letter-like symbols, strings of letters, strings of letters/some beginning sounds, and so on.) Put students' pages together to make a collaborative book. Have children work together to come up with a title. Send the book home with a different child each night so that families can take a peek at their children's early writing success.

Mary Dill and Nancy Areglado, Rolling Valley Elementary School
Fairfax County, Virginia

Child of the Day

This getting-to-know you activity lasts for as many days as there are children in your class—and results in a set of collaborative books that children will delight in reading again and again. The activity works well because it promotes reading and writing using information the children are very familiar with—themselves!

On Day 1, I select a child by pulling a name out of a hat. I explain that every child will have a chance. Each student asks this child one question about herself—for example, "What's your favorite book?" "What do you like to do most in school?" "What's your favorite color?" "Do you have a pet?" As the child answers, I record responses on chart paper. I use the writing experience as a chance to teach skills incidentally. For example, I might ask, "How should I begin this sentence? Yes, I start with a capital letter. How should I end it? Yes, with a period." I follow up by inviting children to write (or dictate) their own notes to the child of the day. They might share something about themselves ("I have three cats too!") or a compliment ("You tell good jokes."). Place the pages in a class book, make a cover, and present the book to the Child of the Day.

> Dear Ricardo,
> I bet your cat would like my cat. They both like to sleep all day.
>
> > Your new friend,
> > John

Karen Sullivan, George Washington Elementary
Mt. Vernon, New York

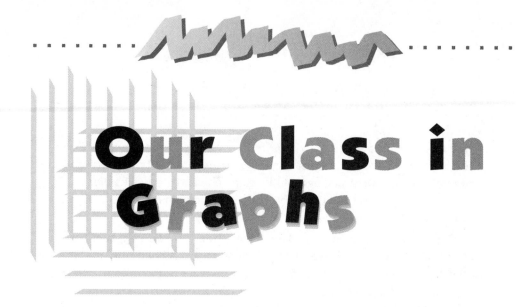

Our Class in Graphs

On the first day and those that follow, bring children together for data-collection activities that will help them get to know their classmates. ("We both come to school on the same bus." "*Pocahontas* was yucky." "My favorite movie is *Cinderella*." "You have three sisters? So do I!") In the process, you'll help children appreciate similarities and differences among one another and get math skills off to an engaging

Numbers in Your Name

Help students learn one another's names with a graph that looks at numbers, too. As a warm-up to the activity, share *Chrysanthemum* by Kevin Henkes (see page 13). Write the name *Chrysanthemum* on the board and count the number of letters in it. Ask: How many letters do you think are in this name? (Then count them.) Does anyone have a first name with this many letters? More than this many letters? Give each child an index card. Have children write their names on the card. Write the numbers (however many letters the longest name has in it) on cards and tack them up in order along the bottom of the bulletin board. One at a time, have children put up their names above the number that corresponds to the letters in their names. Use the graph to initiate discussions about the data:

• Who has the longest name? The shortest name?
• How long are most names?
• How many names have fewer than ten letters?
• How many names have more than five letters?
• How many names have between one and three letters? Four and six? Seven and ten? More than ten?
• What do you think would happen if we graphed nicknames?
• What do you think would happen if we graphed first *and* last names? (Try it!)

Students who are ready to go further can find and discuss an *average* number of letters in a name. As a line-up extension, have students line up according to letters in their name—for example: "If your name has two letters, line up. If your name has three letters, line up." For a challenge, indicate a range: "If your name has between seven and ten letters line up." Or work with division: "If your name can be divided by two with no letters left over, line up. If your name can be divided by three with no letters left over, line up."

How Do You Get to School?

For a first- or second-day activity, let children graph how they get to school. First, have them draw pictures of the way they get to school—bus, bike, feet, subway, and so on. (Have them all use the same size paper.) Set up columns to represent the various modes of transportation. Have children place their pictures on the graph to show how they get to school. (If pictures are on the large side, you might make your graph on the floor or set up a horizontal orientation on a wall in the hallway.) Ask questions to guide children in interpreting the data:

After hearing the Edith Bauer story This Is the Way We Go to School, *children make a graph of how they get to school.*

• How many children take a bus to school? Get a ride? How many walk?

• Do most of the students in our class walk or take some other form of transportation?

• What does this graph tell you about where most students live?

Try graphing the information in other ways, for example, with a pie graph. For a literature connection, see *Where Are You Going, Manyoni?*, page 10.

More Class Graphs

Your students will get even more out of their class graphs if they are involved in selecting graph topics. Have a brainstorming session in which you invite students to suggest data about themselves that they'd like to collect and graph. Post the ideas near your class graph, and choose from among the ideas each time you start a new graph. Suggestions to get your list started include:

• How many people are in your family?
• What is your favorite movie and/or TV show?
• What kind of milk do you drink? (skim, whole, chocolate, etc.)
• What is your favorite kind of cookie?
• How many brothers and sisters do you have?
• Have you lost a tooth yet? (Or graph the number of teeth lost.)
• Have you had chicken pox?
• Who is your hero?
• What month were you born in?
• What is your favorite season?
• How old are you?

Hot or Cold?

Get a feel for how well your students can analyze and interpret information by graphing temperature the first week of school. While you're at it, start a dictionary of weather words (or synonyms for *hot* and *cold*) on chart paper. Check the temperature together the first week. Ask: "Do you think it will be warmer at the same time for the rest of the week, cooler, or a mix of both?" Create a graph to record the temperature. Each day ask, "What do you notice about the graph?" (Make notes based on these questions: Can children fill in information on the graph correctly? Can they read the graph at the end of the week? Can they make predictions based on their findings?) At the end of the week, compare data gathered with predictions.

TIP

For a birthday graph that doubles as a display, see page 63.

T·e·a·c·h·e·r S·h·a·r·e

Gobble-Up Graphs

I give out fish-shaped crackers, round crackers, and oval crackers for snacks. Before we eat them, we create a graph: Which cracker is your favorite? Children indicate their choices on a graph, then gobble up their favorites! For variations, try serving— and graphing—different fruits or vegetables as snacks.

Linda Cardoza, Ascarate Elementary
El Paso, Texas

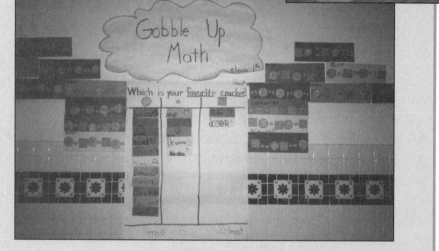

Collaborative Graph

Make a back-to-school connection with the whole school by setting up a giant graph in the hallway outside your classroom. Cover a large space with craft paper and set up the graph sections. (You'll probably want to set up a horizontal graph to accommodate large numbers.) Decide on a data-collection question and write it on the paper. Provide squares of paper and markers for students to record data on the graph. (They can write their names on the pieces of paper and tape them up in the appropriate sections.) Some interesting questions students of all ages can investigate include:

• How many times have you moved since you started _____ grade?
• What's your favorite subject? (lunch, recess, math, literacy, and so on)
• What's your favorite school lunch?
• What's your least favorite school lunch?
• What color are your eyes?
• Are you: Taller than 48 inches/48 inches or shorter?

What statements can your students make about their schoolmates? Write statements about the data you gather on sentence strips, and post on the graph. Notice how the results change as more children record their data.

Stackable Graphs

Turn those small milk cartons students get in the lunchroom into stackable graphs. (Get a few extra milk cartons from the lunchroom for children who need one.) Start by rinsing the cartons. Fold them in at the top and tape down to create cubes. Have children make their first stackable graph by using the cartons to indicate milk choices. (How many children chose skim milk? Whole? Chocolate?) Now have children cover their cartons with colorful paper (or paint them with tempera). Ask them to write their names on the cubes and use them for other graphing activities.

Information in a Box

Quantity graphs let children interpret information by looking at the number of responses in a box. This is a fun graph to set up at the start of the year because children can just write their name in the appropriate box to record data. To set up a quantity graph, make a box for each choice being graphed.

For the first week, try a quantity graph that looks at children's comfort in the class: "I recognize some kids in my class." "I don't recognize anyone in my class." (You can act quickly on this to help children meet new friends. In fact, play an icebreaker game after graphing this information, then regraph! For icebreakers, see pages 21–28.) Other quantity graphs that can help children get to know one another include: What's your favorite season? (Divide a large square into four and label fall, winter, spring, summer.) Which book did you like best? (Label each square with a book you've read the first week. You'll gain helpful information on children's opinions about authors, illustrations, genres, and so on.)

Classroom Brighteners

Bulletin boards, borders, and other displays say a lot about your classroom. Make your walls work for you with the ideas that follow. Each involves children in the display and invites them to keep on using it long after it's up. You'll find bulletin boards that celebrate children and their successes, charts that encourage kindness, and mind maps that help students make smart choices. You'll also find a selection of Venn diagrams that will help your new students get to know one another and develop organization skills they can use all year in the process.

A Friendly Feel

One of my first-week goals is to create a familiar environment for children. Displays about and by them that say "This is your room" include a hallway bulletin board with their photos; self-portraits displayed on class walls (see page 19); and cubby, closet, and table name tags. Seeing their photos, artwork, and names around the room help children feel they belong and give a new room a friendly feel.

Randee Mandelbaum
P.S. 6
New York, New York

Bulletin Boards

Something Special About Me

This bulletin board makes children feel special and provides lots of opportunities for them to get to know one another too. Start by inviting children to bring in something from home that represents them, such as a soccer ribbon, a souvenir from a summer trip, a favorite photo, a letter or postcard from a special friend, and so on. Create a display with the items, making sure to post children's names prominently next to their items. Encourage children to talk with one another about the items on the board. ("Great soccer ribbon! Are you playing soccer this year?")

What do the items say about each person? How many different class-mates do students have something in common with?

T·e·a·c·h·e·r S·h·a·r·e

All Aboard the Reading Express
We build reading excitement right from the start with a board that lets children add a car to a train each time they read a book. To prepare, I make a train car template, copy it for students, and tack one up on

the board. I place copies of the train car, along with markers and scissors, at a work table nearby. To start the board, I share a book with the class and then record the title, author, and something we liked about the book on a train car. Children take over, adding cars to the train each time they read a book. Soon there's a train winding its way across the board. (You can let it wind its way across the walls in your room, too.)

Judy Meagher, Emily Dickinson School
Bozeman, Montana

I Can

Talk to students about things they do well. Are they outstanding spellers? Super skaters? Fantastic at math? Ask children to draw pictures of themselves wearing T-shirts. Have them illustrate something they do well on their "shirts," such as ride a bike, make new friends, read, or swim. If you like, have children design their "I Can" T-shirts on T-shirt shapes cut from paper. Use the pictures to create a beginning-of-the-year display. Reinforce the idea of "I Can" by recognizing other things children are good at: "Danielle, you are good at listening to what others have to say." Provide extra "blank shirts" so that students can add to the board as they become confident at new things.

TIP

For more ideas on building interactive bulletin boards that are just right for the start of the year and beyond, see the *Interactive Bulletin Boards* series (*Math, Language Arts, September to June*) by Judy Meagher and Joan Novelli (Scholastic Professional Books, 1998). For bulletin boards plus poems, playlets, games, and more, see *Super Start-the-Year Book* by Meish Goldish (Scholastic Professional Book, 1991).

Pocket Surprise

Welcome your students back with a bulletin board that holds a different surprise each day. You can be in charge of surprises the first week. Students can team up to take over after that—creating little surprises to share with their new classmates. Directions for building your board follow:

1. Cover a bulletin board with colorful craft paper.
2. Add a sign: Back-to-School Surprise
3. Tack up an open envelope to make a "pocket" for each student. Write each student's name on an envelope.
4. Each day, surprise your students with a surprise in their envelopes, such as:
   • a note welcoming each student to class

- a joke
- a bookmark
- stickers
- a puzzle to solve
- a personalized assignment, such as, "Jason, can you find five things that start with the first letter of your name?"
- the title of a book you think each child might like to read
- an invitation (for example, to hear a special story)
- a blank mini-book
- an award certificate ("Congratulations on learning every class-mate's name this week!")

5. After the first week or so, students can take over this board, teaming up to come up with ideas for pocket surprises. Have students check their ideas with you first, then work together to place a surprise in each classmate's pocket. This might be a poem they especially like, a riddle, a picture, a compliment—the possibilities are endless!

Giant Venn Diagram

One way to let children share information about themselves during the first week—and anytime—is to create a large Venn diagram on a bulletin board. Change the categories every couple of days to keep the activity fresh.

- Cover a board with craft paper. Tack up yarn to form two or three large interlocking circles.
- Use sentence strips to label each circle. Choose statements that students can easily respond to about themselves. For example, for a two-ring Venn diagram, you might start with "I like thunderstorms" or "I have a dog."
- Tack up a basket (plastic fruit baskets work well) of stick-on notes and pens.

- For the first Venn diagram, have children write their names on sticky notes, then guide them in placing the notes in the appropriate circles. Help children see that if both statements apply to them, they will put their stick-on notes in the section where the two circles overlap. (In some cases, they will write their names on the stick-on notes and leave them outside the circles if the statements don't apply.)
- Guide children in a discussion about the Venn diagram. How many children like thunderstorms? How many like thunderstorms and have a dog?

More Venn diagram ideas follow.

Graphic Organizers

Put-Ups

The opposite of put-downs, put-ups let children verbalize ways in which classmates show kindness. Set up a chart to record put-ups. Invite children to add to it when they would like to recognize a classmate's kind act. Read the entries aloud periodically to reinforce the value of children helping one another.

My Kind Classmate	Put-Up	Signed
Fran	finding my stuffed animal	
Ricardo	lending me his markers	
Mr. Jackson	fixing a chair that was broken	

Mind Map

Also known as a semantic map, a mind map is a graphic display of information. As a beginning-of-the-year activity, a mind map can be used to remind children of acceptable behavior in various situations at school. For example, if students tend to be a little rowdy in the lunchroom, we might try a Lunchtime Talk mind map to remind children of topics they can talk about with friends at the table. (See example.) Having a visual reminder can help keep conversations positive and cut down on arguing, fighting, food-flinging, and other unacceptable lunchroom behavior.

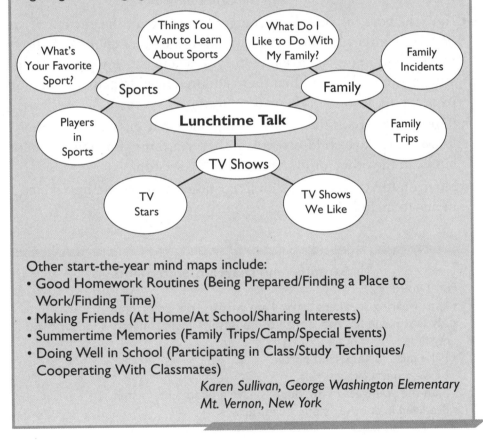

Other start-the-year mind maps include:
- Good Homework Routines (Being Prepared/Finding a Place to Work/Finding Time)
- Making Friends (At Home/At School/Sharing Interests)
- Summertime Memories (Family Trips/Camp/Special Events)
- Doing Well in School (Participating in Class/Study Techniques/ Cooperating With Classmates)

Karen Sullivan, George Washington Elementary Mt. Vernon, New York

Step Into the Circle

In *Super Graphs, Venns & Glyphs* (Scholastic Professional Books, 1995), Honi Bamberger and Patricia Hughes suggest introducing Venn diagrams by making two large circles on the floor with yarn (each circle a different color). They have children sort themselves in the circles by boy, girl. They move on to overlapping circles, having students sort themselves by different criteria. Directions for introducing two overlapping circles follow:

- Label one yarn circle *boy* and the other *brown eyes*.
- Have the boys in your class arrange themselves in the circle that says *boy*. Have girls with brown eyes stand in the other circle. Ask: If you're a boy and you have brown eyes, where can you stand? Guide students to understand that these children need to stand in the overlapping section of the two circles.
- Repeat the activity, this time labeling one circle *girls*, and the other *brown hair*. Have children explain their reasoning for standing in one circle, in the other, or in the overlapping section.
- Move on to Venn diagrams on large pieces of paper. Sample statements to include follow.

Sample Venn Diagram Statements

For Two Rings:
- I am wearing sneakers today. I am wearing the color blue.
- My first name has more than three letters. My last name is longer than my first.
- I like milk. I like peanut butter.
- I have a pet. I like animals.
- I am the youngest in my family. I have a brother or sister.
- I've lived in another state. I like snow.

For Three Rings:
- I like rain. I like thunder. I do not like lightening.
- I'm at least five years old. I've lost at least one tooth. I've had chicken pox.
- My favorite color is blue. I'm wearing blue. My name starts with B.
- I always read before I go to bed. My favorite author is Tomie de Paola. I like to write stories.
- My birthday is in the summer. The month of my birthday has more than four letters. The day of the month I was born on is greater than 10.

T·e·a·c·h·e·r S·h·a·r·e

Three-Ring Organizers

I give each child a three-ring Venn diagram then have children form groups of three. Each child writes his or her name on a line next to a circle, then students in each group talk about what they did over the summer. If all three students

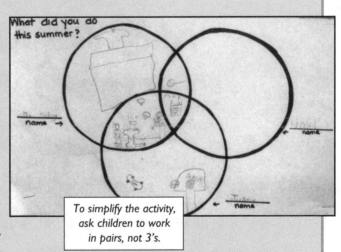

To simplify the activity, ask children to work in pairs, not 3's.

did the same thing—for example, went to the beach—they would write that activity in the intersection of all three rings. If two children did the same thing, but not the third, those two children would write the activity in the place where their two circles overlap. If a child did something that neither of the other children did, that would be written in the part of the circle that doesn't overlap with the other circles. Additional guided

questions for this activity include:
- How many people are in your family?
- Do you speak more than one language at home?
- Who was your teacher last year?
- Do you have a pet?

Students can copy the three-ring Venn diagram as many times as they like to record new information. When students are finished, bring them together to share their results.

Shoshana Jacobs, P.S. 163
New York, New York

Other Displays

Birthday Line-Up

Whether it's a day or a few months away, most students eagerly antici-pate their birthdays. This display is a colorful reminder of all your stu-dents' special days and doubles as a way to teach months, days of the month, chronological order, and more. Start by string-ing a clothesline from one corner to another. Give each child a piece of sturdy paper. Have children write their names and birthdays on the paper and then

decorate them. Give each child a clothespin. Have children work together to pin up their birthday cards in order—starting with the first month of the school year. Once the birthday cards are up, use them to teach math mini-lessons—for example, ask: How many days until [child's name]'s birthday? How can we figure that out? How many days ago was [child's name]'s birthday? How many children have birthdays before you do? How many have them after you?

Happy Birthday to Us

This birthday graph doubles as a display. Cut out a piece of oaktag in the shape of a layer cake. Divide into three "layers," and let children decorate with swirls, flowers, and other festive shapes. Write "Happy Birthday to Us" at the top, then write the name of each month on the cake, four per layer. Give each child a birthday candle. Have children take turns placing their candles on the cake (use tape or reusable wall adhesive) and signing their names next to them. Guide children in reading the graph by asking:
• How many children were born in [month]?
• How many of your classmates were born in the same month as you?
• Do more children celebrate their birthdays in the first half of the year or second half?

Helping Hands

Class jobs are a part of most classrooms. Invite your students to help make a job board by tracing their hands on sturdy paper and cutting them out. Have children write their names on the hand shapes, and tack them up around the board. Make signs for each job—for example, plant caretaker, paper collector, line leader, messenger monitor, and so on. Have children tack up their hands next to the signs when it's their turn.

We're Here Even When We're Not!
When my students are absent, all we have to do is look around our room to see them. As a beginning-of-the-year activity, I have children help each other trace their bodies on butcher paper. They cut them out and then fill them in with words and pictures that say something about them. They use yarn, fabric scraps, and other art materials to decorate their cutouts, then we display them around the classroom so that every child is with us even when absent!   *Rita Wilcox, Fort River School*
Amherst, Massachusetts

Class Quilt

Set up a framework for a class quilt by tacking up a quilt-size piece of butcher paper on a wall. Give each child a "quilt square," a 10-inch piece (or whatever size you choose) of drawing paper. Have children write their names on the squares and draw self portraits. Guide children in arranging their quilt squares on the butcher paper. They can add strips of colorful paper between squares (horizontally and vertically) as well as a quilt border. Other beginning-of-the-year ideas for students' quilt squares include:

• Have children draw pictures of their families on quilt squares.

• Invite each child to depict a favorite activity.

• Help children cover their palms with paint (lightly) and press them on quilt squares.

• Ask children to cut out pictures from magazines that represent things they like. Have them use the pictures to create a collage on their quilt squares.

Leave the quilt framework up all year. Change the squares to make connections with almost anything you teach!